Prompt
Response
Poems of 2014

Ruth Y. Nott

Chiefland, FL, USA

© 2014 by Ruth Y. Nott

To obtain copies of this book or obtain required permission
for use of material herein, email author at
nottruth@yahoo.com.

ISBN 10: 0986279218
ISBN 13: 978-0-9862792-1-8

Published by Envision Books
Printed in the United States of America.

Cover photo – My great granddaughter Tova and her
Mother Amy MacKenzie

Acknowledgements

Special thanks to writersdigest.com and Robert Lee Brewer's Poetic Asides blog therein for nudging my poetic imagination each April and November with the daily prompts they provide. Additional thanks to George Smith for copying those prompts over to the PoemOfTheDay Yahoo group. Without his help posting those as well as the weekly Wednesday prompts the rest of the year, I would surely forget to check writersdigest.com for the daily prompts and write a lot fewer poems!

Table of Contents

2014

This book contains both prompted and unprompted poems. Each prompted poem will have the prompt and date listed before the poem begins.

1-1-14 - Write a weird poem. Maybe it's a twist ending or a person on another planet (or in another time). Maybe it's a land in which weird people are those that look just like us. Or whatever floats your boat.

Isn't It Weird?

Isn't it weird
How you feel let down
The day after the big celebration?
After all the fuss and falderal,
And the mess has been cleared away,
Where is the hope of elation?
Today is just another day,
The first page of another year…
Awaiting your imagination!

1-8-14 - Take the phrase "This Is (blank)," replace the blank with a word or phrase, make the new phrase the title of your poem, and then, write your poem.

Possible poem titles include:
"This Is My Happy Face,"
"This Is the End of the Line,"
"This Is the Last Straw,"
and so on.

This is Ridiculous **(March 18)**

Why am I so far behind?
One poem a week isn't too much to ask
But it seems to be too great a task!

Where have all the hours gone
Which could have been used to write?
Disappeared like ghosts in the night!

How many days were frittered away
Chasing my next great quilt?
I stagger from the weight of my guilt!

It's time to begin another year's work
And make this computer my home
As I put my thoughts into poems.

1-10-14 (Written for a friend in need.)

When Times Are Hard

When times are hard reach within to find
The strength and courage to ease your mind.
Just raise your eyes and raise your voice
In song or prayer - It is your choice;
But speak to Him, as friend to friend
Or patient Father, the two can blend.
He knows your needs and wants to listen
As on your cheeks the tear drops glisten.
He has given you many friends who care,
His angels on earth He wants to share.
So turn your frowns into brilliant smiles
As we hug each other across the miles.
And when times are hard reach within
And reach out to God, your very best friend!

(For Rogie)

1-15-14 - For today's prompt, write a stress poem. The poem could be about something that stresses you (or someone else) out: for instance, ~ death, ~ taxes, and/or ~ Star Wars prequels. Or the poem could be about something you (or someone else) want to stress: for instance,~ your aversion to Star Wars prequels. Of course, you can bend the prompt to your whim.

Am I Stressed?

My dogs are sometimes a trial
My husband can be a pain in the neck
My children are far too distant
My house… never mind…what the heck!
I still have my friends and my faith
I have enough money to get by
My health is good, not a problem
And yet sometimes I still cry
For the fading days of my youth
For the sensuous touch of a lover
For the euphoric high of sweet grape wine
Ah… those days cannot be recovered!
But look at what's yet to come
I'm over the hill and descending
One day before long I'll meet with my Lord
For one glorious and stress-free ending!

1-22-14 - Write an elsewhere poem. Maybe elsewhere is a physical place–like Ohio instead of Georgia. Maybe elsewhere is a season–like summer instead of winter. Maybe elsewhere is a state of mind–like happy instead of depressed. Whatever (or wherever), your elsewhere write it today (and through the week).

Finding Elsewhere

Deep in my mind,
If I dig far enough,
There's an elsewhere
Waiting for me…
Waiting for me
To run out of things
That can't wait
Until tomorrow;
Waiting for me
To realize
I need to slow my pace,
To take a break,
Sit down awhile
And travel deep within;
Waiting for me
To drop my defenses,
Lay bare my soul,
And unwind in the joy
Of Elsewhere!

1-29-14 - Write a building poem. It could be about an actual building, such as the Sears…err…Willis Tower in Chicago or Fallingwater house in Pennsylvania. Or it could be about building something, such as a mashed potato replica of Devils Tower in Wyoming or a papier mache mask.If you can build another interpretation, go for it.

Building Faith

Have you ever watched a child progress
From babe to young adult?
They stumble at first to get to their feet
But they're running before you know it.
They jabber in unknown tongues
Until speech and language are mastered.
They have doubts about what they're told
They question their teachers and parents
As they become responsible adults.
That's how we learn as time goes by
And the same concept is applied
To our growing in trust and faith.
We stumble at first with belief
In a concept often hard to accept.
We jabber and can't find the words
As we learn the fine art of prayer.
We question our teachers and pastors
Ever building our faith and dedication
To our loving Lord and Master.

2-5-14 - Write a work poem. It can be about an occupation, working up a sweat, trying to avoid work, or however you wish to take it.

Work in Progress

Our lives are a continual work in progress
The chart of our lives is quite jagged
With peaks of joy and valleys of distress.
We hope that our line keeps climbing
Leading finally to our success
But we never know how the market may turn…
Will we take a dive or be blessed?
We are a work in progress, our futures yet unknown
And only God can say if we'll pass the final test.

2-9-14 – (Written for my great-granddaughter)

Thinking of Tova

In pictures on the internet
I see your radiant smile
And your rosy chubby cheeks
As your laughing eyes beguile
Looking out across the miles
       that stand between us.

But life may often bring a tear
To slide gently down your face
And that's when I'd like to be there
To hug my Tova Grace;
But there's way too many miles
       that stand between us

(Continued on next page)

You are a miracle of God
Who formed you in the womb,
Who molded you with His own hands
And placed in your heart a tune…
A lullaby to bridge the gap
that stands between us

If I could hold you close
And whisper in your ear
I'd speak of love and butterflies
To soothe and ease your fears
But there's just too many miles
that stand between us

So if you'll listen with your heart
To hear this grandmother's voice
And feel my hugs by proxy
You'll hear it was not my choice
To have all those many miles
that stand between us

And as you grow from year to year
And keep building upon your faith
Granny Ruth will still be sending
Loving prayers for Tova Grace…
For if we each take one of God's hands,
He'll close the gap between us.

2-12-14 - Write a hair poem. It could be all about hair or hair accessories. The poem could just mention hair in passing. Or you could write an ode or eulogy to a specific hairstyle.

Dog Hair

Long silver threads
Adorn my winter jacket –
Sasha is shedding

2-19-14 - Write a handheld poem. Whether it's video games, smart phones, or soft tacos, the world is filled to the brim with things that can be held in one hand (or both).

Touching God

Holding a baby
In the palm of your hand
Is like touching God

2-26-14 - Take the phrase "My (blank)," replace the blank with a word or phrase, make the new phrase the title of your poem, and then, write your poem. Possible titles might include: "My Sharona," "My Two Left Feet," "My My My," "My Little Prince," and so on.

My Way of Thinking

My way of thinking may not agree with yours,
But I reserve the right to think as I please.
Your way of thinking may not agree with mine,
But respecting your right to your thoughts is the key
To living in harmony with each other.

We are individuals with freedom of choice
But carefully consider the choices you make
For there are consequences to our every action
Choose wisely for any thoughtless mistakes
May hurt not just you, but another!

3-5-14 - Write an announcement poem. Either document the announcement of someone else, or share your own announcement. Announcements can be true, fictional, or somewhere in between.

Zzzzzzzzz...

Coming soon – nap time!
My eyes are drooping lower
Slowly closing...Zzzzzzzzzz

3-12-14 - Write a care poem. As with many of the prompts, a care poem can be handled (with care) in many different ways: write a poem in which you care about someone (or something); write a poem about a caregiver (or care receiver); write a poem about the Care Bears; or if you don't care about anything, let that guide you.

Galations 1:10 KJV

"For do I now persuade men, or God? Or do I seek to please men? For if I yet pleased men, I should not be the servant of Christ."

I care about my family
I care about my friends
I care about the earth
And the horrid shape it's in.
I care that we're so careless
We let each other down
When we should show our love,
Compassion can't be found.
So are we really truthful
When we say we really care?
Or are we just performing
On the stage that we all share?

.

3-25-14 - Write an excited poem. Of course, I'm a bit excited about the upcoming challenge–in a good way. But excited can manifest itself in plenty of other ways as well, including feeling sick, scared, or upset.

We're Pregnant!

Long awaited news
Home pregnancy test confirms –
Hallelujah!

(Not me folks!)

4-1-14 - 1. Write a beginning poem. Today is the beginning of this challenge. It's also the beginning of April.But there are so many other beginnings: Beginning of a relationship, beginning of school, Beginning of the rest of your life, and so on. Pick a beginning to write about.   -or-

2. Write an ending poem. Often, though not always, beginnings come as the result of an ending. Sometimes endings are cause for disappointment, heartbreak, or numbness. Other times, endings are celebrated. Capture an ending today.

Pain and Joy

With tears in their eyes
Mother and baby first meet –
Pain and joy embrace

4-2-14 - Write a voyage poem. A voyage can happen in a variety of ways–even on foot, or psychologically. Heck, the process of writing a poem is a sort of voyage all its own.

Voyager

Adrift on a sea of memories
Alone with the wind and the waves
The painful take flight on the wings of gulls;
Wrapped in sunlight, the best are saved.
Rocked like a babe in the womb
I succumb to the sway of the sea,
Asleep in visions of yesterday
As each wave brings you back to me.

Adrift on a sea of memories
Awaiting the coming storm
When the gulls will take refuge beside me
And the pain that they carry transform
My sunlight to darkness and turmoil
As lightning streaks turbulent skies
Illuminating my guilt and my shame
And the fear lurking deep in my eyes.

Adrift on a sea of memories,
Alone as the storm subsides,
Hearing their cries as the gulls depart,
I awake drifting home on the tide.
Reality shakes the awakening
As dream ships and waves disappear.
Today takes shape in the morning mist,
A new voyage surprisingly near.

4-3-14 - Write a message poem. Messages can be delivered in a variety of ways: postcard, e-mail, text message, letter in a bottle, smoke signals, secret codes, jumbotron proposals, etc. Also, messages themselves can be simple, complicated, nice, mean, happy, sad, and so on.

Nag, Nag, Nag...

Okay, I get the message!
You don't have to go on and on.
I made a mistake and I'm sorry.
Finally the light has dawned.
You better believe it won't happen again,
Not in a million years!
(And if it does you'll never find out
'cause Baby I'm outta here!)

4-4-14 - Take the phrase "Since (blank)," replace the blank with a word or phrase, make the new phrase the title of your poem, and then, write your poem.

Since Then...

Do you remember when
We used to drive down to the lake
And lose ourselves in kisses
Oh so sweet and deep?
Back then we were making memories
And vows we couldn't keep...
I miss those days of innocence,
But a lot has changed since then.

Do you remember when
We drove to Freemont Lakes
Fished and played games with the kids
Beside the flickering firelight?
Or clung together frightened
Through those stormy Nebraska nights?
I miss those days when we were close
But so much has changed since then.

Do you remember when
Our lives had changed so much
That I begged to be set free
When all I really wanted was to stay?
Why didn't you fight to keep me?
Why did you let me run away
Not knowing how much I'd miss you
In all the years since then?

4-5-14 - Write a discovery poem. The narrator could dis-
cover: an object, a person, an animal, a dishonorable deed,
or any number of things. You can focus on the discovery,
examine the aftermath, or even just mention it in passing.

Discovering Truth

I should have seen it
But you wove your web so well
Your lies blinding me

Pulling me inside
Entangling me, choking me
Killing my spirit

Leaving me lifeless
Unable to move beyond
Your web of deceit.

4-6-14 - Write a night poem. Vampires and werewolves? Cool. Clubbing and saloons? You got it. Lovers together alone? Right. Ex-lovers alone on their own? Sure thing. You figure out your night poem–and, yes, (k)night poems are fine too.

Girl of My Dreams

Dark as the night were her eyes,
Bright as the day was her smile,
Soft as the gentle rain her voice.
The warmth of her touch electrified
The love within my heart.

The darkness of night became her.
Moonlight enhanced her glow.
As she walked the stars shown brighter
And the owls refrained from "who"ing
For fear she might depart.

But where is she now this enchantress –
Whisked away by the morning mist,
Chased away by the morning light,
And I close my eyes in utter dismay
Willing the dream to restart.

4-7-14 - Write a self-portrait poem. Pretty straightforward, right? That doesn't mean there's not a lot of room for creativity. Just look at artists and their self-portraits; there's a lot of differences in the self-portraits of Kahlo, Schiele, Dali, Van Gogh, and others–and not just because the artists look different themselves.

Self Portrait

I am old...
No longer the beauty,
No longer slim,
No longer energized,
No longer ambitious.
I am old.
Thinning gray hair,
Overweight but losing,
Tired and weary, drained,
Lacking motivation.

I am old.
Where do I go from here?
Will you lead me?
Time marches on.
I am older.

4-8-14 – Write a violent poem. Could be person on person violence, person on animal, animal on animal, nature on person/animal/nature, and so on (insects, erosion, cosmos, etc.).

– or -

Write a peaceful poem. I suppose this might be the opposite of a violent poem. But perhaps not.

Peaceful

Stretched out in the sun
Absorbing its warm rays –
Canine morning nap

4-8-14 –

Social Camouflage

Life goes on around me – without me,
Acknowledged yet ignored.
I am surrounded by activity and chatter
Yet isolated by my own silence,
Invisible to most, alone in a crowd.

4-9-14 - Write a shelter poem. Shelter might be a structure like a house, apartment, or hotel. Shelter could be a tent or cardboard box. Shelter could be an umbrella, overpass, cave, or car. Shelter could be a state of mind, part of a money laundering scheme, or any number of interpretations.

In the Shelter of Your Arms

Jesus,
My Lord,
From high on the cross
You beckon and I come,
A sinner, to the shelter of Your arms.

Resting,
Recovering,
Regaining my balance
I am safe in the shelter of Your arms.

Opening,
Embracing,
Held close to your heart
I am comforted in the shelter of Your arms.

Loving,
Forgiving,
Providing grace to the lost
I am saved by the shelter of Your arms.

4-10-14 - Write a future poem. The future might mean robots and computer chips. The future might mean pocalyptic catastrophes. The future might mean peace and understanding. The future might mean 1,000 years into the future; it might mean tomorrow (or next month).

Mercedes Concept Car (Photo seen on a Facebook post)

Once upon a time, in a land far away
A wizard began his usual day.
"Let's look to the future," he told his class,
"And see what one day may come to pass.
As your crystal balls begin to cloud,
Look deep inside and make me proud."
"I'm beginning to see it," one young man shouted.
"Look there, a new car!" And no one doubted
For there it was, all shiny and sleek
As they all gathered 'round to take a peek.
Its windows, like wings… " Delorian!" they called.
"Not at all," said the boy, somewhat appalled.
"Check the insignia!" he said with surprise
It was a Mercedes they all realized.
Its trunk was unusual for the whole lid lifted…
And then their attention was suddenly shifted.
"It has no steering wheel! I don't believe it!
How do they drive it… or even conceive it?"
"I know," said Jane. "Look, it's so neat!
There's a joystick right there between the seats
So you can drive this car like a game!"
"Who would have thought," the wizard exclaimed,
That the day would finally come
When driving would be so cool and so fun!

4-11-14 - Make a statement the title of your poem and either: - a. respond to or b. expand upon the title. Some example titles might include: "A Date Which Will Live in Infamy;" "Guns Don't Kill People, I Do;" "This Is Your Brain on Drugs;" "Smile for the Camera," and "Be Kind Rewind." Of course, there's an incredible number of possible titles; pick one and start poeming

"I Have a Dream..."

I have a dream,
A dream of a new world order,
A world in peace and harmony
Where countries have no borders.

I have a dream
Where love and fellowship rule,
Where the natural thing is doing what's right,
And leaders refuse to duel.

I have a dream,
But it's just a dream
And it haunts me night after night,
A dream of a world redeemed!

4-12-13 - Write a city poem. The poem can take place in a city, can remember the city (in a general sense), be an ode to a specific city

City

C onstant noise
I ncreasing crime rate
T raffic jams
Y ear-round bedlam

4-13-14 - Write an animal poem. Pick a specific animal or write about your animal spirit. Maybe you'll get tricky and write about mustangs (meaning the car) or jaguars (meaning the American football team). Maybe you'll do an acrostic, or even go crazy and write a sestina (crickets).

(See 4-28-14)

(Sometimes I find that a poem may fit into two or more categories and, when I'm running low on ideas, I sometimes use one poem to cover two prompts as with this one.)

4-14-14 – Take the phrase "If I Were (blank)," replace the blank with a word or phrase, make the new phrase the title of your poem, and then, write the poem. Possible titles might include: " If I Were President," "If I Were Smarter," "If I Were a Little More Sensitive," or "If I Were Born on April 14."

If I Were Smart...

If I were smart
I'd make better use of my time.
If I were smart
My poems would be sublime.
If I were smart
I'd read more books.
If I were smart
I'd not worry how I looked.
If I were smart
I'd find more time to pray.
If I were smart
I wouldn't work, I'd play!
If I were smart….

4-15-14 - Write a love poem. Love, it's such a big 4-letter word that can mean so much to so many for a variety of interpretations. Friendly love, sexual love, dorky love, all-encompassing love, jealous love, anxious love, love beaten with a baseball bat, hot love, big love, blues love, greeting card love, forgiving love, greedy love, love in a music video, and so on and so forth.   -or- Write an anti-love poem. Well, kinda like love, but take it back the other way

Luvulots

As technology continues
To invade our daily lives
It changes how we think and act
And often how we survive.
Those spoken words
"I love you!"
Or a signature
"Love, Mom"
Somehow seem outdated
And need to be revived.
"Luvulots"
"Luvu2"
What other combos
Might I do?
Those lengthy conversations
Or letters from your kids
Are now on Skype or email
Or on your Facebook page
Along with private thoughts
(made public)
And (God forbid) our age!

(Continued on next page)

It's funny how our habits change
As we learn a brand new language
Of abbreviated, run-on words
Or throw up our hands in anguish
At the gibberish we've contrived!
I guess it doesn't matter
As long as we still "talk"
And don't lose track of love
Along technology's walk.

4-16-14 - Write an elegy. An elegy doesn't have specific formal rules. Rather, it's a poem for someone who has died. In fact, elegies are defined as "love poems for the dead" in John Drury's The Poetry Dictionary. Of course, we're all poets here, which means everything can be bent. So yes, it's perfectly fine if you take this another direction–for instance, I (Brewer, that is) once wrote an elegy for card catalogs.

(See 4-4-14)

4-18-14 - Write a weather poem. A weather poem can be a poem about a hurricane or tornado; it can be a poem about the weatherperson; it can be a poem about forgetting an umbrella on a rainy day; it can be big; it can be small.

Weather Woes

It's funny how the weather seems to change
Making our days so very up-endable!
Oh, I wish God would somehow arrange
To make weather a bit more dependable!
The weatherman can only give guesses
About sunshine or rain or the snow
And even he must sometimes confess
There are some things he just doesn't know!

4-19-14 - Pick a color, make the color the title of your poem, and then, write your poem. You can make your poem black, white, red, purple, turquoise, puce, or whatever your heart desires. And the subject of your poem can cover any topic–as long as you've plugged a color into the title.

Red

Red on the outside
Chocolate on the inside –
Addictive candy!

Green

M & M mascot
Commercially appealing –
Salesman of the year!

4-20-14 - Write a family poem. I've actually written a few poems about my family this month already, but you don't have to restrict yourself to your own family. There are any number of human families, of course, but also animals, insects, and other organisms. Plus, there are "families" of other types as well.

Who Is Your Family?

Sometimes it's hard to count
The members of my family.
But they all belong to me
Of that I have to doubt.

Across these United States
My family is scattered
But we all know that love
Is the only thing that matters.

And certainly another family
I have are my church friends
And on their love and support
I know I can always depend.

Some others are stitched together with love –
These would be my quilting sisters.
We're one for all and all for one..
You don't want to mess with us mister!

(Continued on next page)

And there's the folks I worked with for years...
We still share a very strong bond
We still keep in touch and we care
Though most have retired and moved on.

Of course each and every one of us
Are a part of the family of man.
Guided by God in our daily lives
According to His holy plan!

4-21-14 - Write a "back to basics" poem. For me, back to the basics means jumping to the fundamentals. Maybe it's me re-learning (or practicing) fundamentals–like running or writing–but it could also be a child learning how to tie his shoestrings, which can be a unique experience for both the child and the adult trying to give instructions and advice. Back to basics could also be re-setting a state of mind or getting back into a routine.

Conundrum

Sometimes when I'm quilting
I want to rush along,
Forget to press a seam
Or use thread that isn't strong.
Perhaps I didn't square it right
Or my seams are a bit too wide.
Sometimes it seems like little wrongs
Are just too big to hide!
That's when I have to stop and think
"Now how did Lois do it?"
'Cause back to Beginners Class
She said it was easy, "Nothing to it!"
But many years have come and gone
Between those days and now
Old age has made my fingers ache
And I can't remember how
To do the simplest little things
The way that I was taught.
So what the heck am I going to do
With all this fabric that I bought?!

4-22-14 - Write an optimistic poem. The glass is half full – or - write a pessimistic poem. The glass is half empty.

Anticipation!

Jesus is coming
Unexpected, in the clouds –
Oh, glorious day!

4-23-14 - Write a location poem. Location could be physical such as: the Laundromat, a public park, a glacier, a flying saucer, etc. Or location could be emotional, psychological, metaphysical, or some other kind of word that ends in -al. Or surprise everyone

Panic Attack

Under the doormat,
Back in the car,
Inside the trunk,
Under the stars,
Beside the bed,
Near the sink…
Oh, my head!
I just can't think!
Dump out my purse,
And fall to my knees
Oh thank you Lord!
I just found my keys!

4-24-14 - Take the phrase "Tell It to the (blank)," replace the blank with a word or phrase, make the new phrase the title of your poem, and then, write the poem. Possible titles include: "Tell It to the Hand," "Tell It to the Judge," "Tell It to the Six-Foot Bunny Rabbit," and so on.

Tell it to the North Wind

Tell it to the North wind.
Tell it to the moon.
Tell it to the weatherman,
"It must stop snowing soon!"
Tell it to the plow man.
Tell it to the icy street.
Scream into the blizzard,
"When will winter be complete?!"
Tell it to the North wind
Blowing cold and strong
"I'm tired of all this ice and snow!
Blow it back where it belongs!"

4-25-14 - Write a "last straw" poem. Everyone encounters situations in which they decide they're not going to take it anymore (whatever "it" happens to be). It could be a loud noise, an abusive partner, someone taking the Pop Tart but not throwing the box away, or whatever. Write about the moment, the aftermath, or take an unexpected path...

Thirsty

Who took the last straw?
The container is empty!
I can't drink my coke!

A sip and a slurp
A drip and a dribble
Hey! This ain't no joke!

Who took the last straw?
I gave it a try but
This old one is broke!

4-26-14 - Write a water poem. Life depends upon water, so there are any number of ways to write this prompt. A few thoughts that jump to mind include pollution, rising water levels, hurricanes, fracking, surfing, fishing, swimming, rain, drinking

Water

Water
Flowing out
Filtering down
Rejoining the earth
Precious liquid life-blood
Nourishing our plants
Home for the fish
Rain for crops
Water

4-27-14 - Write a monster poem. There are the usual suspects: zombies, vampires, werewolves, and mummies. But monsters can take any form and terrorize a variety of victims.

A Friend with a Gun

You don't need the movies anymore
To be frightened by evil and rage.
You need only to watch the TV news
Or read the newspaper's front page.
Our children are the demons and monsters
Without need of a writer or script.
They are plotting and planning their moves
As their bullets and knives are ripped
Through the bodies of fellow students…
Victims of mad, twisted minds
And no one knows why they do it.
They can't see the clues or the signs.
How can we be raising such monsters?
Are we blind to their needs and their pain,
Unable to see how they suffer
And just cannot deal with the strain?
We need to pay more attention.
And listen to what they won't say.
I know parenting is no easy task
Ask for help if there's no other way!
Our schools should be places of safety,
Places to learn and have fun,
Not tremble in fear for your life
When you're facing a friend with a gun!
Dear Lord, I pray for your mercy
For your healing of their spirits and minds.
Without you there is no hope for our children
And their demons will win every time.

4-28-14 - Write a settled poem. Settled can be a good, relaxing thing; settled can be an accepting something that wasn't your first choice thing; settled can be coming to a stop; settled can be pioneers in a strange land; and so on.

Eagle

Gliding on currents
Of air, feet extended,
He descends to land.
Silently touching
Toe to branch and folding
His wings he awaits
The slightest movement
In his far sighted vision –
Reading the menu.

4-29-14 - Write a realism poem. A poem that is rooted in the real world. Or…Write a magical poem. A poem that incorporates magical or fantastical elements.

(See 4-28-14)

4-30-14 - Write a "calling it a day" poem. Some people might call this "Miller time," others may refer to it as "closing time."

Midnight

I think I'm ready to call it a day.
The sun is long gone
And tomorrow's anon.
The crickets are chirping out in the field,
Squirrels have bedded
And night bugs are headed
To dance in the street lights glow.
This day has ended
As the hours have wended
To the tick, tick, tock of the clock.

5-7-14 -Ttake the phrase "The Boy Who (blank)," replace the blank with a word or phrase, make the new phrase the title of your poem, and then, write your poem. Feel free to replace the word "boy" with "girl."

The Boy Who Loved Dragons

The roar of the dragon,
The fire of his breath,
The speed of his wings
Outdistance the rest.
With pencil to paper
The legend becomes real
For the boy who loved dragons
Their life-blood can feel.
It soars through his veins
With an arc and a swirl
And onto the paper
Dragons tumble and twirl
In dances as ancient
As time without end
Though some fall to heroes
Who hunt and defend.
Yes, the boy who loved dragons
Creates quite a world!
In his imagination
Their offspring are curled
In dark caves on mountains
Awaiting their turn
To take to the night skies
And villages burn.
For the boy who loved dragons
They are real and alive
Just waiting and watching
As he helps them survive.

5-14-14 - Write a poem in which the unexpected happens. Could be a good unexpected–like receiving a gift from an anonymous person; could be a bad unexpected–like having someone break into your house; could be a confusing unexpected–like having a complete stranger propose marriage.

Unexpected Perfection

They're not really unexpected,
Those Florida afternoon storms
Thunder and lightning and hail
Have always been the norm.
And then there are days which surprise us
All sunny and bright blue skies
When we are treated to the perfection
Of God's handiwork visualized!

5-21-14 - Write an object poem. Pick an object and write about it. Or pick an object and make it a central piece of your poem. Or pick an object and make it the title. Or pick an object and write an acrostic. Or come up with some other way to combine an object with your poem.

Selfie!

Staring down at me,
Ready to share life's moments –
Camera lens clicks!

5-28-14 - Use a new(er) word in a poem.
Merriam-Webster recently added 150 new terms to its collegiate dictionary, including tweep,

Progress?

I did sign up for Twitter
But I don't think I'm a tweep.
I have a house full of e-waste
And narry a broom to sweep.
Maybe if I tried some gamification
My housekeeping skills would bloom
Or perhaps a little crowdfunding
Could pay a maid to clean my rooms!
I don't know the reason for hashtags
But perhaps it's to garner #attention
To your latest selfie photograph
Or some brand new digital invention.
The computer age marches on
I can't stop it, don't you see?
The big data keeps on growing
Without any help from me!

6-18-14 - Write a TV-inspired poem. It can be a poem about a game show, a talk show, a news show, or an entertaining series. The poem can be about commercials, remote controls, or having the biggest/best entertainment system in town. The poem can be about contemporary TV, or it can go old school.

What Did You say?

I used to wonder why
Old women were hard of hearing,
But I've learned the awful truth
As my old age is nearing.
It's not our fault you know
We can blame it on our men.
Just like with everything else
It's their fault in the end.
They lose their hearing long before
Ours begins to fade
And blast the TV way too loud
'Cause they won't wear their hearing aides!!
They spend four to five thousand dollars
On a tool to improve how they live...
And then leave it sitting on the shelf
Because batteries are too expensive!
Meanwhile their wives must try to repeat
Everything they cannot hear
So they can make some little sense
Of the shows which they hold dear.
And little by little we grow like them
Old and hard of hearing
Wondering why the folks on TV
Are whispering when they should be cheering!

6-24-14 -

Friendship's Release

Friends will come and friends will go
And sometimes there's nothing left to show
Of loyalty, fairness and devotion.

Friendships are a lot like love affairs.
You fall in deep and might not be aware
That the other is feeling a totally different emotion.

Months go by or maybe years
Before your eyes open and begin to clear
And you wonder why such a big commotion

Over little things you once accepted as "everyday"
And thought of them only as just "their way"
Now irritate and seem to point to your own promotion

Of distance and escape and a little peace
And the tide is turning towards friendship's release
As the storm clouds clear o'er a tranquil ocean.

6-25-14 - A word association prompt. - I'm going to list some words below, you pick one (or more) and use to write your poem. The word does not have to appear anywhere in the poem or title, but it's totally fine if it does. Here's the word list: • toast • pop • right • paper • howl • little

Pop!

The Toast goes "Pop!"
It just won't stop
Even with talk
Of plagiarism
By Snap and Crackle's box!

It's the right thing to do,
"We're going to sue!
You just can't steal
Our famous Pop
We'll serve the papers on you!"

Then with a howl
Little Toast cried "Foul!"
And the trio was forced
To drop the suit
When the judge said "Nope, nohow!"

6-29-14 -

Are You Seeking the Lord Or...?

Are you seeking the Lord?
Have you found Him yet?
Are you satisfied with how things are?
Do you yearn for more, have any regrets?

Don't be a spectator as you walk the path...
Go help your neighbor to carry his load
Seek ye the lord and practice His ways,
Learn His commandments and follow the code.

Are you seeking the Lord?
Have you lost your way?
Sinner repent and turn towards home!
God is looking for you, His beacon displayed.

The Light of His Son shines on the way!
Seek ye the Lord as he seeks for you.
Open your heart and let Him come in.
Abide in His presence for a life renewed!

7-6-14 -

Fever for Jesus

A fever for Jesus is rising inside
As the fire of the Spirit burns in my heart.
My mind is ablaze with love for the Lord
Striving each day this love to impart.

Fervent in prayer, and continual praise,
Praying BIG prayers and expecting to see
My prayers realized by His holy will.
I have faith in His promise of uplifting me.

Sheltered by His arms, comforted by His love,
I will glorify God for all He has done
While burning to share his good news with my friends,
I'm ablaze with the fever for Jesus, His son!

7-8-14 - A Golden Shovel poem from "Café Comedy" by Robert William Service using each of the words in his line "and I forget I'm no more young and fair" as the end words in each line of my poem.

Deceptive Reflections

I stare into the mirror and
See the wrinkled old woman I
Have become. I cannot forget
The age spots and gray hair. I'm
Unable to see the beauty within – No,
Only the vision of failing health and more
Painful infirmities unknown to the young.
We are born in pain and die in pain and
Are slow to learn that life is just not fair.

7-8-14 - A Golden Shovel poem from "A Song of Life" by Ella Wheeler Wilcox using each of the words in her line "Come out in the sun while I teach you the secret of life" as the end words in each line of my poem.

Invitation

I invite you to come,
Put away the old. Come out
Into the bright new day in
Christ. Push away the
Clouds of doubt and sun
Yourself in His warmth while
His everlasting Word I
Proclaim and begin to teach
His way and start to show you
How sweet life can be in the
Shelter of His arms. No secret
This, but a familiar old story of
Love, sacrifice and eternal life.

7-8-14 - A Golden Shovel poem from "Café Comedy" by Robert William Service using each of the words in his line "falling in love just from a photograph" as the end words in each line of my poem.

Puppy Love

Spiraling, spinning, falling,
And rising again in
A whirlwind of first love,
Enthralled by the thought of just
One tiny little kiss from
That mysterious boy only seen once in a
Friend's tattered photograph.

7-8-14 – A Golden Shovel Poem from "Where the Side-walk Ends" by Shel Silverstein using each of the words in his line "There is a place where the sidewalk ends" as the end words in each line of my poem.

A Folded Flag

Standing bravely there
A young woman is
Crying, holding a baby and a
Folded flag, remembering the place
Under this same tree where
Once they had kissed and now the
Color guard retreats down the sidewalk,
Her heart breaking as the service ends.

7-9-14 - For this week's prompt, take the phrase "Blame (blank)," replace the blank with a word or phrase, make the new phrase the title of your poem, and then, write your poem. Possible titles include • "Blame it on the Rain," • "Blame Yourself," • "Blame the Bad Guys," and so on.

Blame it on my age

If you don't see me posting
My poems or Facebook chatter
Don't worry that I'm ill
Don't wonder what's the matter...
    Just blame it on my age!

Each day begins with plans
For writing, cleaning and sewing
But usually I'm stuck wondering
Just where the hours are going...
    Just blame it on my age!

The value of each moment
Is lost with each distraction
Nothing ever gets finished
I find no satisfaction...
    Just blame it on my age!

And when I pause to say my prayers
As each day turns into night
I may not say "Amen"
Until the early morning light...
    Just blame it on my age!

(Continued on next page)

I will drift from prayer to dreaming.
Toss and turn, get up and roam
Or put my restless thoughts to paper
Hoping they become a poem...
      Just blame it on my age!

They say these "senior moments"
Are a symptom of senility.
They rob you of your patience
And sap all your abilities...
      Just blame it on my age!

Haven't heard from me in ages?
Well now you know just why
It's not because I'm ill
Or because I didn't try...
      Just blame it on my age!

7-16-14 - Write a poem in which you imagine a story for/about a stranger. Maybe someone you see on public transportation, a couple at the laundromat, or a neighbor. Is the person more fabulous than expected? Fallen upon harder times? Exactly as one might guess?

The Hermitage

We used to have a neighbor
Living across the way
Who we liked to call "the hermit"
Who was disappearing day by day
Behind a growing hedge –
Her unkept and dense protection
From others' prying eyes,
But not from their projections
Of just what was going on
Inside that greenery stronghold.
Our imaginations ran the gamut
From "just shy" to "hidden gold!"
We never did find out the truth
And one day she moved away.
The "For Sale" sign now reads "Sold"
And we're all waiting for the day
When new owners take up residence
Behind that wall of green
And we wonder if they'll cut it down
Or remain among the unseen!

.

7-30-14 - Write an outside poem. And (physically) get outside if at all possible. Now, the poem itself can be about the great outdoors, but it can also be about other iterations of the outside concept: * thinking outside the box, Or getting outside: * the cubicle, * the bedroom, * the hospital room, * depression, * addiction, * your head, * your heart, * your comfort zone

Where the Wildflowers Bloom

There's a place along the path
Where wild petunias bloom.
They crowd out other flowers…
Don't want to give them room
To show their pretty faces
To the early morning sun.
Years ago I planted Petunias
Over near the patio
And every year since then
They wander to and fro
Popping up across my yard
Here and there, one by one…
Or in pink and purple profusion
All together in a horde
Waving brightly in the breeze
As if to greet the Lord
And thank Him for their freedom
As they bask there in the sun.

8-3-14 –

Lead or Follow?

Are we being the person God wants us to be,
Or are we just following the crowd?
Do we keep our faith all to ourselves,
Or do we shout it out loud?
Will we be a warrior for the cause of God,
Or turn our backs and run?
Let us always remember to never give up
On God and His precious Son!
David fought Goliath alone
While the king's men stood at length
Eleazar fought the Philistines alone,
Right to the end of his strength.
These mighty men of God stood tall
Doing God's will in battle.
They didn't just follow along with the crowd
Acting like a herd of cattle.
So we must consider our actions today
And listen for God's command.
We must be the leader He wants us to be
Spreading His Word 'cross the land.

8-12-14 – (Rewrite of Gentle Spirit ©2011)

Gentle Spirit

Gentle spirit spread your wings.
Your home awaits in eternal spring.
Do not look back or to life cling.
New life awaits, new hope I bring..
Some tears will flow and some will grieve;
But have no fear for those you leave.
I will lift them up, make right the wrongs;
For your loving heart has made them strong.
So come my child as the angels sing..
Gentle spirit, spread your wings!

8-13-14 - For this week's prompt, write an upside down poem. Of course, the poem could be about something (or someone) being physically turned upside down, but it could also be a symbolic reversal of the roles or change in how things are commonly done. Or you can just write a poem, print it out, and yes, turn it upside down.

Oops!

Life is a struggle
Flailing legs and gaping mouth –
Overturned turtle

8-20-14 - Write a news poem. When I'm really in a creative rut, there's one constant source of new ideas for me: the news! There are the big headlines; there's the sports page, the comics, and the advertisements.

News of the Day

The news of the day is this:
It ends as it began...
Restless and sleepless,
Foiled by circumstance.
4:00 am the dogs awake
And bark at a passing car.
My eyes refuse to close again
Until the evening draws nigh;
But though they could
And I wish they would
The TV's too loud to allow it
11:07 and hubby's still up
Enthralled by western movies.
My bed on the couch is empty.
I've escaped to my own little world...
Alone, as usual, with my sewing machine,
Catching up on writing my poetry,
Or playing computer games.
My eyes would like to close again
As the morning begins past midnight
But though they could
And I wish they would
The TV's too loud to allow it.

8-27-14 - Write a malfunction poem. Yes, he says, "I changed today's originally planned prompt to fit today's circumstances. Sometimes you just gotta have that kind of flexibility."

However, not everyone handles malfunction the same: • some roll with the punches, • some throw punches, • some throw fits, • some quit, • some try again, • and so on. Plus, there're any number of malfunctions out there: • wardrobe malfunctions, • mechanical malfunctions, • and heck, I think many of my poems suffer a malfunction or three.

Clueless

Okay everybody, I give up!
I'm without a clue or hint.
That danged printer is at it again –
It just refuses to print!
It may be out of ink again.
That seems to be a common woe,
Or the paper may be jammed.
That's the way things seem to go.
Sometimes it skips a page.
Sometimes it prints too many.
If you've got a solution please tell me
Because I just don't have any.
Looks like it's time to go shopping
But first some research is due
For I'll want to get the very best
When I replace this old printer with new!

9-3-14 - Write a framily poem. That's not a typo. I'm thinking framily: friends and family (you know, like Sprint's framily phone plan?)... Write a poem that involves (or is inspired by) your friends and family. Everyone should have a good story to tell, whether it's funny, sad, serious, etc.

Framily Ties

We are tied to life with a silver cord
And to each other with hugs and love.
Our children are tied to our apron strings
And our faith ties us to the Lord above.
The ties of friendship are soft but strong,
Cords of kindness and understanding.
Some say we are tied to our jobs
But jobs can be way too demanding.
Old lovers are tied to our heartstrings
With memories sweet and unending.
Our framily ties may be strong or weak
And may often fray and need mending.
So thread your needle with faith and love
And sew forgiveness into each stitch.
Your framily may become a patchwork
But your heart and soul will be rich.

9-10-14 - Write a messing around poem. There are a number of ways to take the phrase "messing around," and I expect y'all will explore that territory well. For me, I'm going to write and get back to messing around.

Just Messing Around

A long and dreary rainy day
Can seem to sap your strength away.
Ambition stirs, then takes a break
Your eyelids droop – can't stay awake.
Nothing takes shape, no chores, no plans
You're just messing around, no demands.
The sun peeks out for a moment or two
But soon disappears along with the blue
Of promising skies and hope renewed.

9-21-14 –

Pray First

We must turn to God in everything.
This is what we know as trust.
We must have faith that our Lord above
Is loving and kind, yet just.
We must pray to God for others
Pray *first*, our faith to renew.
Don't wait until our prayers
Become *the least* that we can do.
Pray unceasingly and pray everywhere.
Turn to Him before anything else.
Then allow Him and his earthly team
To repair lives and provide good health.

9-24-14 - Write a "next in line" poem. This could be a poem about somebody waiting in a line at the DMV or the grocery store obviously. But it could also be about a line of lovers, a line of errors, or a line of poetry. What is coming up? What is around the corner? These could be topics for a "next in line" poem.

Next in Line

Next in line – Relax!
Close your eyes and breathe.
A little meditation time
A lot of stress relieves.

Next in line – Try reading
To distract your mind from today.
Lose yourself in make believe
And your troubles will drift away.

Next in line – Take a nap!
Fluff your pillow and stretch out.
See how many prayers you can say,
Or how many sheep you can count

Next in line   Arise!
Take care of your body and soul
Or next in line may be ill health
As you are growing old.

10-1-14 - write a broken down poem. write about: • cars,
• lawn mowers,• or the human spirit.

Bell Massacre

She broke down when they closed the last casket.
Her tears ran like a California flood…
An unending torrent of grief.

All the hugs and love that surrounded her
Could not soothe her tormented soul
Or bring on a moment's relief.

A daughter and six grandchildren lay sleeping…
Lying silent in seven satin lined boxes
A sleep of forever without end.

There's no comfort for her anguished spirit,
No justice for the souls of the dead,
No way for her heart to mend.

Murdered by their own troubled grandfather
Who then took his own worthless life…
An impenitent coward's way out.

She will never again hear their laughter
Nor watch her grandchildren at play.
Even her faith is in doubt.

(Continued on next page)

Dear Lord, give her strength for her journey.
The way back will be long and hard
With pitfalls along the way.

Please don't let her life remain broken.
Send your angels to be her guides.
And just love her is all I pray.

10-8-14 -Write a natural poem. Write about the natural world (plants, animals, etc.); write about all-natural foods or diet; write about human nature or animal nature; or write about nature vs. nurture. Those are just a few ideas. Go with whatever feels natural.

It Just Comes Naturally

Somehow some people seem
To take the time to talk and dream
To find the pictures in the clouds
And say their prayers right out loud.
It just comes naturally.

Some people lie and some people steal
To them a life of crime is real
And punishment does little good
When they come right back to the "hood."
It just comes naturally.

(Continued on next page)

Somehow some people lend a hand
Or bake a cake or change their plans
To help someone in desperate need
And never take credit for their deeds.
It just comes naturally.

But other folk just think of "Me"
And just can't ever seem to see
Another's pain – Can't make the connection
When blinded by their own reflection.
It just comes naturally.

Now wouldn't this world be a better place
If we could change the human race...
Make hate and bigotry and crime decrease
And do away with war since love and peace
Would just came naturally?

10-15-14 - Write a pick up poem. In the poem, you could write about picking stuff up–like operating a crane or cleaning a bedroom. Or it could be about picking up someone at a bar. Or picking up the pace. Or whatever else you happen to pick up…on. Have fun!

Pick Up Sticks

There used to be a children's game…
And there probably still is –
We called it "Pick Up Sticks,"
A game of skill for sure.

But these days the term "pick up sticks"
Has a totally different meaning
As I walk around my yard each day
Admiring Mother Nature.

Many trees adorn the landscape
Dropping their twigs and branches
All along my walking path
Especially after a hard rain.

I try to "police" my mowing route
To keep them out of the blades.
And bending is good exercise
So I guess I shouldn't complain!

10-29-14 - write an emerging poem. Some things emerge out of the shadows or the darkness. Some things emerge from the water. Others emerge in broad daylight, whether we're talking monsters, athletes, politicians, or what have you. Poems themselves emerge from the blank page and/or screen (or our own subconscious)

Eclipse

Moonlight on the water fades
Into darkness...
Silence descends
Like a shroud until
  Slowly
     Slowly
A glimmer of a halo
Outlines the moon's rebirth
As it emerges full again,
Its reflection dancing
Across the restless waves.

11-1-14 - Write a game over poem. Our family spent a couple months putting together a haunted house in our garage for Halloween, and now that the holiday passed, so I've got a bit of that game over feeling. People who play video games know about game over. And people who play other games, whether baseball, Monopoly, or poker. There's a moment in every game at which it is game over–except maybe Minecraft, (which may be why it's so popular for so many).

Football

Florida Gators –
Seems like the game is over
But wait… maybe not!!

11-02-14 - Write a together again poem. It's one thing to split up; it's something else to come back together again. Sometimes getting back together is a good thing; sometimes it's a bad thing; and sometimes it's just awkward.

Together Again

Sometimes, no matter good intentions,
We find ourselves straying
From the straight and narrow path.

We forget about our promises
To love and praise the Lord,
And seem bound to tempt His wrath.

But if we truly loved Him once
He still waits with open arms
Ready to forgive if we just ask.

When we're together once again
With our savior by our side
We can look to the future, not our past.

For a truly repentant sinner
Enjoys a special sheltered place
Where he can rest within the Master's arms

Relearning the proper way to live,
Pulling himself together again
While protected and safe from any harm.

11-3-14 - Write a blanket poem. In my part of the country, we've had a recent cold spell and folks have been cuddling up under their blankets. In other places, they've even had to deal with a blanket of snow. Some people–regardless of the weather–have their security blankets, which may or may not be actual blankets. And some folks make blanket statements. There may be other ways to cover a blanket poem and if you know it, then go for it.

The Second Blanket

I love to find a pattern
And pick out the fabric to use.
I cut and sew for hours
But I'm doing what I choose.
Sometimes I sell a quilt
Or give one to a friend.
They'll keep you warm in winter
On that you can depend.
My husband has a special blanket
Which he pulls up to his head
And a second one neatly folded
Lying at the foot of the bed.
Now the temperatures are dropping
And last night he needed two
But pulling up that second blanket
Is such a chore for him to do
That he'd rather go on shivering
And then make a great big show
Of complaining I have the temperature
Set down way too low!

Superhero? Nah!

One doesn't have to be a superhero
To make a difference in this world.
You just need to watch and listen
For opportunity to knock.

Perhaps you can say a prayer
For a neighbor in distress
Or pick up a little trash
On your walk around the block.

Take some time and clean your closet
Bag up your good old clothes
And take them down to Goodwill
Or to a Hospice store.

You can write a note or send a card
When you hear someone is ailing.
Or pick up the phone and call your mom…
You know you should do that more!

Visit your local nursing home
And cheer a lonely soul.
Read a book or say good morning
And offer a comforting hug.

To them you will be super
And a hero they will praise.
You just might come to like it
And catch the volunteer bug!

11-5-14 - Take the phrase "Keep This (blank)," replace the blank with a word or phrase, make the new phrase the title of your poem.

Keep This Going

Keep this going if you can.
Click "Like" and "Share"
Or "Copy" and "Paste."
See how far it can travel
Across the World Wide Web…
It just can't go to waste!
There's a story in a book,
A real tear-jerker you see.
It's a tale of love and loss –
Of a tiny babe in a manger,
Of a persecuted Savior
Who died upon a cross.
He tried to teach the way of love.
He taught kindness and compassion
But was betrayed by one of His own.
He was called the Son of God
And by His death He paid our debt
And invited us into His home.
So keep this going if you can
Click "Like" and "Share"
Or "Copy" and "Paste"
See how far His story travels
Across the World Wide Web.
It must not go to waste!

11-6-14 - Write a happy now poem.

Comfort Food

Chocolate galore –
Yummy to the core,
Cherry cheesecake
Buy or bake,
Banana split,
What a hit!
Peanut butter and jelly,
Makes a big fat belly!
Donuts and cinnamon rolls
Pecan pie, half or whole!
Load 'em up, fill my plate
I'm so hungry I just can't wait!
I ate it all! I don't know how…
But you can bet I'm happy now!

11-7-14 - Write a compulsion poem. On Sundays in autumn, I often feel a compulsion to check how my fantasy football team is doing over and over again. When I was younger, I often felt a compulsion to play Tetris–something about stacking up all those lines.

(Continued on next page)

The "Busy Bug"

I have a compulsion to stay busy.
Guess you could call it the "Busy Bug."
It attacks me early in the morning
And lasts the whole day through.
I just cannot sit idle
When there's just so much to do.
If I start a paperback or an e-book
I feel guilty that I'm sitting still.
The "Busy Bug" is relentless.
It nudges me all day long.
When I try to rest for a moment,
The bug says that move is wrong.
I don't know how to control it.
There's no vaccine that will work.
I just go from one job to another…
From housework to computer to quilting.
I just cannot sit idle
If I do, I start to feel guilty.
There's yard work to do and groceries to buy.
The list is endless it seems…
Feed the dogs and take out the trash,
Take a bath and wash my hair.
If you can help me stop all this madness,
I'll do anything, go anywhere!
I'm supposed to be retired
And living a life of leisure,
But that just hasn't worked out!
That danged "Busy Bug" won't leave me alone
I get not a minute of peace
He's the reason I'm writing this poem!

11-8-14 - Write a blind poem. Three blind mice, blindfold-ed, "She blinded me with science," "Houston in the blind," "Blinded by the light..."and so on.

Dawn

Blinded by the light
I stumble into the morning
Shaking sleep away

11-9-14 - Look to the news and write about something re-cently reported. It doesn't have to be something today, but something in the past week or month would be ideal. There's always good and bad things happening in the world, and poetry is a powerful way to document events.

Biobots

Have you heard about biobots?
Robotic bugs with a purpose,
Crawling into tiny little spaces
To listen or see what's what.

They are search and rescue's latest tool.
They can go where dogs cannot go.
They may not be as sweet and loveable,
But some say these cyborgs are cool!

(Continued on next page)

I'm not sure, though, how I'd react
Lying wounded and trapped below ground,
If I was approached by a rescue roach…
I might end its career with a WHACK!

So perhaps we should rethink the biobot
And not make it some loathsome insect.
For, although it may be just right for the task,
A sweet and calming companion it's not!

11-10-14 - For today's prompt; • take the phrase "(blank) Trouble," • replace the blank with a word or phrase, • make the new phrase the title, • and write.

Stomach Trouble

Yesterday was my husband's birthday.
Happy 86th and many more!
Yet he didn't feel much like celebrating
With nausea down in his core.
Nevertheless he tried to look happy
Through dinner, drinks and dessert.
But I knew it wasn't going to end well
When his stomach continued to hurt.
It seems exciting events make him nervous
And this brings another day to mind
A day from a long time ago,
After we said "I do" and signed on the dotted line.
Let's just say it was a honeymoon interrupted
By stomach trouble gone berserk!
It's a night I try not to remember…
A wedding night without any perks!

11-11-14 - Write a timely poem - Or-   Write a timeless poem.

The Golden Rule

"Do unto others as you would have them do unto you." –
A very timeless adage it's true.
But so many want to change it, abusing these precious words.
I'm sure you may have heard:
"Do unto others *before* they can do unto you."
(But don't forget that they can sue!)
"Do unto others as they deserve having done unto them."
(Judging is God's duty. Let's leave that to Him!)
You can switch the words around to however your boat floats;
But I prefer the words that Jesus wrote:

Matthew 7:12 – *"Therefore all things whatsoever ye
would that men should do to you, do ye even so to them; for
this is the law and the prophets."*

11-12-14 - Write a poem for and/or about something that cannot be seen. I mentioned cold, but there are so many more possibilities, including love, gravity, future, thoughts, and sound waves. Our lives are filled with things we know exist but which we can't see.

Those Who Believe

They say you are there
And yet you are not.
We are told to believe
In what we can't see.
Trust in your faith.
Think outside the box.
Believe in the man
And the God he must be.
He lived and he died
Just as all men do
And then reappeared
To encourage his friends.
He promised redemption
And hope to renew.
He promised that one day
He'd be back again.
For two thousand years
He hasn't been seen,
Except in the actions
Of those who believe,
Those who remember
And on him do lean,
Who trust in his promise
And his blessings receive.

11-13-14 -Write an optional poem. I'm thinking of how some things in life are completely optional; in fact, most things are.

Eternal Life

Whether you go to Heaven
Or spend eternity in Hell
It all depends on you.
Whichever path you take
Works out as you
Meant it to.

God gave us freedom of choice…
We can believe in Him or not.
For me, I choose eternal life.
With Jesus as my guide,
Following Him
Is easy to do.

11-14-14 - Write a follow poem.

Thanks George!

Following your lead
Writing a poem each day –
Poetry challenge

11-15-14 - For today's prompt, • take the phrase "Holy (blank)," replace the blank with a word or phrase, make this your title. Think of this as the "Robin prompt" from the old Adam West Batman TV show, because Robin would always make exclamations that began with "Holy,"

Holy Stupidity!

I was sitting at a traffic light
When fire trucks came along
Lights and sirens blaring
Quite a distressful song.
The light was red in his direction
The other guys had green
But the cross traffic wouldn't stop
For that frantic emergency team!

Holy stupidity!
Are they deaf to the siren's sound?!

It seemed to take forever
For those trucks to make their way
Blaring and flashing and honking
Through that intersection today.
I hope those folks who wouldn't yield
Don't find themselves in trouble
For then they just might realize
That karma could burst their bubble!

Holy stupidity!
What goes around comes around!

11-16-14 - Write an explanatory poem. In dozens of creative writing courses in college the mantra is, "Show, don't tell." Well, today's prompt is sort of different–in a way–in that it's a tell poem, or explaining poem, though how and what you explain may vary a great deal.

November 19, 2015

Let me tell you how I'm feeling
And then we'll see how it goes.
Let me look at my thermometer
And tell you what it shows.
It's reading 28 degrees
And to me that's really cold
For my arthritis is telling me
I'm truly growing old.
My knee and hip are aching
And I'm shivering in my shoes.
I've wrapped myself in blankets.
What else could I do?
It's not supposed to be this cold
In America's Sunshine State,
But I heard the weatherman say
This is a record breaking date!
Oh well, today will pass.
It's Florida after all –
And tomorrow it will be 75…
A warm and lovely Fall!

11-18-14 - Two prompts today: • Write a sweet poem. Or
• Write a sour poem.

Sweet Tooth

If it isn't loaded with sugar
It's offensive to his taste.
It matters not how hard I worked
It's going to go to waste.
It doesn't matter what his doctor says
For he's a privileged man.
"I can eat whatever I want.
I'm old and that's my plan!"
He doesn't care if it makes him die
Because he's "ready to go."
And I'm sure he'll enter those Pearly Gates
With a bag of candy in tow!

11-19-14 - Write a poem about: • making excuses, • listening to excuses, or hey, • maybe excuse someone for making them.

Excuses! Excuses!

Get a grip!
Zip your lip!
No more excuses!

Get it done.
Have some fun.
See what it produces.

Let's not wait,
Not hesitate.
We've waited long enough.

No more pacing
No more placing
The blame on other stuff.

The time has come
Don't act dumb
You know just what I mean!

It's up to you
To see it through
And wipe the whole slate clean.

11-20-14 - For today's prompt: • take the phrase "I'll Never (blank)," • replace the blank with a word or phrase, • make the new phrase your title • and then, write.

I'll Never Forget

So many years have passed
Yet you're still on my mind…
The warmth and spark of desire
That from your eyes did shine…
The tenderness in every touch,
The thoughtful things you did…
These are the things I cherish
When I find my thoughts amid
Days of long ago passion denied
And left to slowly disappear
Into a wisp of leftover longing
In a voice which I still hear.

11-21-14 - For today's prompt, pick a direction on the compass, make it your title and write… (Inspired by a painting in my doctor's office titled "West of Key West.")

West

West of Key West
Aqua and azure ripples
Clear blue water

11-22-14 - Write a release poem. Maybe somebody's being released from prison or a contract. Maybe a person is signing a release form. There's emotional and physical release. Animals capturing and releasing other animals. Trees releasing leaves in autumn. And so on.

Release

"Let go and let God"…
Advice to heal your soul.
Forgiveness, release…
Let God take control.
If your burdens are too heavy
Hand them over. Be healed.
Release the weight to Jesus.
He knows your fears are real.
Don't try to carry it on and on
You will stumble and may fall.
Help is just a prayer away.
He's waiting for your call.

11-23-14 - Write an alone poem. Some people covet "alone time." Others prefer not to be left alone. Many like a certain balance. But this doesn't have to just be about people.

(This is a poem I wrote a long time ago and which appeared in my book "Crazy Patch" ©2007 but I am claiming it as my "alone" poem for today!)

Alone

Lonely little caboose on the railroad tracks
Wondering if the train is ever coming back.
How were you left there so sad and forlorn
To watch for the cars and their passing to mourn?
No more smoke, no more whistle, no more clickety-clack,
No more make believe trips to Chicago and back.
The station was busy when Johnny was ten.
You circled the tracks again and again.
Now your tracks are all dusty – your windows the same.
Your little friend Johnny has tired of the game.
The happiest days that you can remember
All came to an end one night in December.
A new kind of track lay stretched on the floor
With shiny new cars… one, two, three, four.
Your Johnny now travels to "Indy" and "Le Mans."
'Round banked curves and hairpins go the cars that he runs.
So exciting the trips to Daytona and back,
That he never even sees you there on your track.
Poor little caboose – no good by yourself.
So sad to be left there alone on the shelf.

11-24-14 - Take the phrase "I'll Be (blank)," replace the blank with a new word or phrase, make the new phrase your title, and then, write. Possible titles include: "I'll Be Back," "I'll Be Late for Dinner," and "I'll Be a Monkey's Uncle."

I'll Be Seeing You

I'll be seeing you
In the wind and the rain,
In the clouds and the shadows
And the wildfire's flame.
I'll be seeing you
In the butterfly's wings,
In the wildflower's bloom
And the birds which sing
Hallelujahs in their praise.

I'll be seeing you
In a baby's smile,
In a mother's love
For her newborn child.
I'll be seeing you
In the homeless man
Trapped in a life
Which wasn't his plan,
But making it day by day.

(Continued on next page)

I'll be seeing you
In the dawn's first light
And the midnight moon
On a haunting night.
I'll be seeing you
For I cannot resist
Finding the Master
In all that exists
In His magical earthly display!

11-25-14 - You have two options: • Write a love poem. –
Or -   Write an anti-love poem.

Impossible!

How can anyone write an anti-love poem?
Our very existence is about love.
We were created by the love of the Father.
We were conceived in an act of love.
We are taught to love one another
As much as we love ourselves.
Who can be against love?
We receive love.
We expect love.
We show love.
Who can be against love
As much as we love ourselves,
We are taught to love one another.
We were conceived in an act of love.
We were created by the love of the Father.
Our very existence is about love.
How can anyone write an anti-love poem?

11-26-14 - Write a same poem. I guess it could be the same old poem, but it could be a completely different poem that looks at a person or thing or system that is still the same. Or maybe a poem about how all people are the same. Or take the "same" concept and show how things are not the same.

Same Old Stories

Repeating those same old stories
Reliving your childhood again
Feeling the same love and hate
You felt so strongly back then.
It isn't good to hold onto the past,
To the hurt and the shame of it all.
The bits of love you remember
Can't compare to the bad you recall.
Why let the past control you?
The past is ever the same.
It's the present day and the future
Where you can control the game;
But even that is hard to accept
Once you've reached a certain age.
When advancing years and declining health
Won't let you turn the page.
You don't want to live in daily pain,
So you return to the past more and more.
It may end up the same for all of us
You never can tell what's in store.
So say a prayer for compassion
From the Lord and all of your friends
Who are forced to listen to *your* tales
Over and over again!

11-27-14 - Write an appreciative poem.

Thank You Lord!

As the years pass
And I look back on my life,
I find I am grateful
For the tears and the strife,
They taught valuable lessons
 I might not have learned
And made precious the days
Of happiness earned.
I find I am grateful
That life can go on
Through children and grandchildren
With whom we can bond.
I find I am grateful
For forgiveness of sin,
For Your love and mercy
And a church to attend.
I find I am grateful
And wish I could repay
The debt that I owe you,
But I know there's no way.
So thank you Lord
For a life to look back on
And for giving me the hope
Of one more bright dawn!

11-28-14 - Take the phrase "(blank) News," replace the blank with a word or phrase, make the new phrase your title, and then, write. Possible titles include: "Good News," "Bad News," "Daily News," and "Old News."

Unwelcome News

The death of a friend,
A pet in distress,
Love at an end,
Failing a test,
Cancer is back,
Dropped your iPhone,
Hole in your sack,
No money to loan…
It may do great harm
This unwelcome news.
It could be your karma
Or maybe a ruse.
We can accept it or bail,
There's no way to know.
Just inhale and exhale
And go with the flow.

11-29-14 - Write a do it again poem. This could be a poem about taking a mulligan or re-doing a mistake. Or maybe re-doing a magical moment. Or a poem for all those folks who like to ride roller coasters and get right back in line.

Never Again

If I should ever find myself
A single gal again,
And someone showed an interest
In making me their friend…
Or expressed a heartfelt love
And offered me a ring…
I think I'd turn away.
And not let my heart sing.
Sometimes love is beautiful
And passion heaven sent
But as the days and years go by
You wonder where it went.
Blinded once, but now you see
The deception and illusion.
I'd rather live a life alone
Than deal with such confusion.
I've walked that road before
Right through to the very end
And I'd rather live a life alone
Than ever do it again.

11-30-14 - Write an inevitable poem. The poem that always had to be, or a poem about something that was inevitable. Maybe two people getting together was inevitable, or maybe two people splitting up was inevitable. But there are so many things that seem inevitable with hindsight.

All Good Things...

Inevitable –
These poems must come to an end.
Good night readers!

www.ingramcontent.com/pod-product-compliance
Lightning Source LLC
Chambersburg PA
CBHW071819020426
42331CB00007B/1541